Dollars Want Me

The New Road To Opulence

Henry Harrison Brown

Transcribed for Women
By Sarah Anne Shockley

Women's New Thought Library

Dollars Want Me: The New Road to Opulence
Henry Harrison Brown, 1903, 1917

Dollars Want Me: The New Road to Opulence
Transcribed for Women

Women's New Thought Library transcribes classic New Thought texts from outmoded patriarchal language into wording specifically empowering to today's spiritual women. References to Mankind, Man, God as He/Him, and the general use of "he" and "him" become either gender neutral or feminine, leaving the remainder of the text as written by the original authors. As a result, these Truths become more accessible and inclusive and, therefore, more potent and life-affirming, for modern women.

www.WomensNewThoughtLibrary.com

Any Road Press, 2020
ISBN: 978-1-947057-02-9

Author's Dedication:
To all who would be free from the grind of labor

This new Law of Henry Harrison Brown's has given me new strength and power such as few could easily realize.

-- 0 HASHNU HARA, Editor of WINGS OF TRUTH, London, Eng.

I believe the idea that money wants you will help you to the right mental condition. Be a pot of honey and let it come.

---ELIZABETH TOWNE, Editor of NAUTILUS.

Money is of no value. It cannot spend itself.
All depends on the skill of the spender.

- RALPH WALDO EMERSON

CONTENTS

Preface by the Transcriber v
Preface by the Author vii
Preface by the Author to 30th Edition viii

Supply 1
Time A Factor 19
Fundamental Considerations 22
Affirmations for Success 36

About the Author 45

PREFACE

As a woman, I have often felt excluded from a lot of the classic books written about money and abundance. Written mostly by men, they were penned in language that is predominantly male-oriented.

I want to believe that these authors had women in mind too, but using only masculine pronouns, referring to God as male. Even though I believed that the principles were, indeed, universal, I kept stumbling over the patriarchal language.

When I read *Dollars Want Me,* I immediately felt it had something of value to offer women in terms of our relationship to money. I loved the idea of turning attention away from *wanting* money, to money wanting *us.*

So, I went through and reworked the book, leaving most of the original wording intact so as not to change the spirit of the transmission, but updating the masculine language into feminine terms.

I find this new women's version very empowering and hope you have a similar experience while reading *Dollars Want Me: A New Road to Opulence for Women.*

- Sarah Anne Shockley, Transcriber

PREFACE
By the Author to the First Edition

To the Reader,
This essay upon the Dollar appeared in NOW as one of a series of twelve lessons entitled, "*Success and how I won it through Affirmation.*"

It attracted much attention and drew out from its readers many letters. This appreciation has decided "NOW" Folk to reprint it in form for a wider circulation.

This well conserves the purpose for which it was written. I wish to awaken my fellows to a sense of their present possessions and help them to a realization of the Principle which controls Life's expression so that, living being to them a fine art -they will cease to look for happiness in some far-off heaven, but will enter into the enjoyment of the one they create HERE and NOW.

It is believed that this little monograph is the first utterance of the thought that each person has the ability so to radiate their mental forces that they can cause the Dollar to FEEL them, LOVE them, SEEK them and thus draw, at will, all things needed for their enfoldment from the Universal Supply.

IT WILL HELP YOU TO RISE ABOVE THE DRUDGERY OF ENFORCED LABOR AND ENABLE YOU TO ENTER UPON THE MANIFOLD EXPRESSIONS OF LIFE WITH THE JOLT AND SPONTANEITY OF CHILDHOOD.

This is the thought that comes to you with this, my Lesson of Success.

HENRY HARRISON BROWN. San Francisco, California, May 1, I903.

PREFACE
to the Thirtieth Edition

The constant and increasing demand for this modest booklet and the beneficent effect which it has had on thousands of its readers, seem to justify its appearance in a new and enlarged form. May it have also a wider influence and an enlarged power to free the minds of its readers from the tyranny of things.

HENRY HARRISON BROWN, San Francisco, California, March, 1917.

Supply

She who dares assert the I,
May calmly wait
While hurrying fate
Meets her demands with sure supply.
- from Helen Wilmans

HARMONY

There is neither health nor prosperity without harmony. There is no peace, no health, where there is want, be it want of material Supply, wisdom Supply or love Supply. Love, Truth and Dollars---these are necessary to a woman's well-being.

Mind, body and estate must be cared for. In order that there may be health, happiness and prosperity, there must be Harmony. This Harmony is found in merely giving Self, the Soul, her way.

Harmony is living in obedience to mental law. It is found in right thinking.

The main cause of the unrest, the dis-ease (the un-ease) that afflicts women is poverty thinking.

Remove poverty by right thinking and all attendant evils will disappear. This right thinking means that there shall be on the part of the individual woman a change of attitude toward the Dollar.

MENTAL ATTITUDE

The prevalent attitude is want for the Dollar, and a belief that Dollars are power. This must be outgrown and the attitude must be that ALL POWER IS IN THE INDIVIDUAL.

Dollars are machines with power delegated to them by people. They are useless without people.

Dollars Want Me! is to be the thought of the new woman. A few so think now and have obtained mastery of Supply.

DEMAND AND SUPPLY

It is a legitimate demand on the part of each woman that she have enough.

To supply your needs is the function of the universe. All is for you. The sun shines for you; the waters run for you; the flowers bloom for you; the grain ripens for you; and the earth teems with beauty for you. All would be useless, would be purpose-less, but for you.

When they cease to be, there is no use for the universe or anything in it. Without you these are virtually non-existent. You alone give a meaning, a use, a value, and a purpose to the universe.

There is enough in the Universal One from which all things materialize, for each woman to have enough to meet all her desires without robbing any.

Infinite Supply is all around us and yet there is want. Whose fault is this? It is not the fault of The One. It is in ourselves. We have not known how to claim, nor have we claimed our own.

LAW OF SUPPLY

The law is simple and it is laid down by the greatest political economist as well as the greatest mental scientist the world has in its historic records.

He was not a theologian, neither did he deal with questions of a future life, as many seem to think; he was a sociologist and a socialist. He dealt with questions of "the life that now is." His name was Jesus. He gave the Law thus: "*Seek first the Realm of the Creator and Its righteousness, and all things shall be added unto you."*

STUDY THE LAW

Analyze the Law thus:
"Realm of the Creator?"
Where?
"*Within you.*"

"*Creator is Spirit,*" he said. "*The Realm of the Creator*"' is then in the Soul. It is the Ego or Soul within you. Know yourself as Soul; know yourself as Spirit---this is the Law.

Live rightly, is the meaning of "righteousness." Live in accord with your sense of right; obey your own conscience. Then all things shall be yours.

Things of whatever kind, of all kinds, are manifestations of the One Substance. Things are, like yourself, manifestations of the one Creator. Dollars are things. Dollars are manifestations of the One Creator.

THE LAW IS SIMPLE

Plain directions, these: Live true to self; live spiritually; give the first place in your thought to the eternal, from which all things come and then all things will come to you at need.

"*First?*" Yes! Not *things* first, but that mental condition which *controls* things. Not Dollars first, but that mental attitude which attracts Dollars.

I TRUST MYSELF

That mental condition is Faith in Self as a manifestation of Omnipotence, Faith in Self as a manifestation of the All-Good, Faith in the Universe as justice, Faith in the Universal One as entirely Good, Faith in the Life You are, to draw Her necessary Supply of things demanded for Her highest expression.

Then let things come. This is all, but it is Creator.

This is the "straight gate." Few there be that enter in, but all may.

THINGS ARE SECOND

Few place things second- Dollars, position, influence, show - these, in common thought, come first. But these are *results* of Power.

First become one with the Power, *become* the Power, and these desired things will come.

The ordinary process of business, the customary method of thinking, is to be reversed. Think from inward Power, think from Being.

BE MASTER

You will then be the Master and things will take their right place. Become "one with the Creator" by recognizing Her as Sovereign in your Soul.

Listen to Her in the edicts of your Soul. If you become negative, say to the Higher in you, "*Now, Creator, do your work your way and it will be done satisfactorily to me.*"

No one can fail when she assumes this attitude of Love and Trust. It would be an impotent Creator, and therefore no-Creator, that did not work when these conditions are made.

POVERTY: HOW CURED

Poverty is a mental condition. It can be cured only by the Affirmation of Power to cure:

I am part of the One and, in the One, possess all.
I possess all!

Affirm this and patiently wait for the manifestation. You have sown the thought-seed, now, like the rancher, wait for the sprouting and the harvest. It can never fail you when, like her, you choose to trust.

CURE OF POVERTY

Repeat this Affirmation, no matter what the

appearances. No matter if hungry, houseless and alone, affirm:

Creator is my Supply. My Supply is Infinite. Dollars want me!

Trust implicitly in the inviolable Law of Cause and Effect. You are Cause; Supply is the Effect that must follow your Affirmation.

AS YE SOW SO SHALL YE REAP

In the past, you have sown poverty-seeds, and are now reaping the crop. You do not enjoy this harvest.

Sow, amid these results of previous sowing, Plenty-seeds and Plenty will come. Supply is yours when you sow Supply-seeds. Sow, no matter how seemingly black the conditions. The seeds have Creator in them and cannot fail.

AFFIRMATIONS FOR USE

MY SUPPLY IS INFINITE, FOR CREATOR IS MY SUPPLY!

SUPPLY CAN NEVER FAIL ME.

Make this your Affirmation and hold it. HOLD IT.

SUPPLY

The Law of Supply is as sure as gravity. In this Affirmation, ALL IS MINE! DOLLARS WANT ME! you have re-polarized your aura. You have changed your vibration and you will draw, as the magnet draws the needle, all you can use.

Try it! Never let go of your trust that Dollars, or that for which they stand, will come.

Thy Realm, 0 Soul, has come and thy will is done for Creator and Soul are One.

"All is mine; 'tis but by asking:
Ere I make my silent plea
Life unlocks her richest treasures
For my waiting eyes to see."

OPULENCE

You conquer fate by thought.
If you think the fatal thought of humans and institutions,
you need never pull the trigger.
The consequences of thinking inevitably follow.
- from Carlyle

THE DOLLAR SIDE

Personal ideals, of necessity, must differ, yet, since money represents objective power, its consideration must enter as a factor into every ideal of success.

Money represents Supply. It stands in our thought, for food, clothing and shelter; for books, pictures and companionship; for enjoyment, unfoldment and expression.

Material Supply is a necessity of Life. The Dollar is the concrete representative of this necessity. But the Dollar also means opportunity for the realization of high ideals.

The individual woman must be free and, until the necessities of life are assured, she is not free.

PERSONAL LIBERTY

THUS THE DOLLAR STANDS FOR INDIVIDUAL LIBERTY.

Personal liberty finds its basis in pecuniary independence. Financial independence and personal liberty bear very largely the relation of cause and effect. We can almost say that in the popular mind the Dollar confers liberty.

In Soul Culture, a mental attitude of superiority to the Dollar results in personal liberty. There is no liberty to one who feels herself limited by the want of the Dollar. Debt is one of the most tyrannical of masters.

Mackay well says:
The debtor is ever a shame-faced dog

With her creditor's name on her collar.

There can be no liberty to one who feels the slavery of debt.

IDEALS OF SUCCESS

Into your ideal of Success, therefore, there must be firmly budded this ideal of pecuniary independence. This independence does not lie in freedom from debt, neither does it lie in large bank accounts nor the possession of property.

Monetary success and personal liberty do not go hand in hand. Indeed the average woman of wealth is truly a slave, enslaved to the necessities that her monetary possessions involve, and a worse slave to her fears.

WHAT IS SUCCESS?

SUCCESS LIES IN THE MENTAL ATTITUDE THAT ARISES FROM THAT SENSE OF PERSONAL POWER WHICH MEETS EVERY CONDITION WITHOUT ANXIETY.

That cannot be called success that results in ill health and unhappiness, unrest or fear. Eliminate these from your ideal and you have, as a necessary concomitant of success, financial ease.

THE NEW THOUGHT

In the old competitive thought, people sought business and wanted the Dollar. Under the New Thought, it is: "*Seek first the Realm of the Creator and right living and all things necessary to my happiness will be added to me.*"

The Soul has only to exercise its drawing power.

When the conscious mind lets itself be led or drawn, it will be drawn to what it desires. Desire is the magnet. Let it have its way.

Trust in your own Love of Truth and Love of Goodness and never question. That you desire it, is enough. That you desire it, is evidence that it already exists for you on the Soul-side.

Be passive to the desire and LET it manifest. This attitude is itself Success.

WHAT TO THINK

Think positively: THINGS BELONG TO ME. I AM ALREADY POSSESSOR. THEY WILL COME TO ME AT NEED.

Then LET them come. If they do not readily come, hold no anxious thought about them.

Having accepted Truth that ALL is mine and that ALL DESIRED CONDITIONS OR THINGS

WILL MANIFEST, keep on working in an equable, confident frame of mind, and LET them come.

Anxiety, doubt, and mistrust show that you have not claimed them as realities but have held them as dreams or possibilities.

Until you hold them as realities, they cannot come.

THE RIGHT MENTAL ATTITUDE

Change your attitude toward business. Do not seek it. SEE IT MENTALLY ALREADY YOURS and LET it come.

Attend yourself to details as they come to the surface. Consider business a Principle that will run, as runs a mountain stream, when you remove your conscious will from it.

All your concern is to be ready to use this business stream as the rancher uses the water as it comes to her ditch.

There is but one Power and that is the Universal, the Infinite Power.

BUSINESS IS POWER

Business is a manifestation of the One Power. Use Power as does the telegrapher: LET it come and then direct it.

The wisdom for the day comes with the day.

LET it come by having faith in Self. Work each moment as if what you desire were here and it IS here.

PLACE OF MONEY

As to money, regard it also as merely the power that keeps business going. Welcome its coming and rejoice at its going. It never does its work until, like water in the stream, it has passed under the wheel.

The hoarded Dollar does not work and is of no real value to you.

The Dollar you spend is the only one you really have, for by the experience of spending it you gain a growth, an enlargement, that is yours forever.

YOU ARE POWER

Money has only delegated Power. *You* direct its expression.

Change your attitude toward money. It is not "the almighty Dollar." Almighty Power *uses* the Dollar.

Say to the Dollar, "*I do not need you. You need me. You are of no use until my brain and hand use you. You wish to be used. You come to me that you may be used. I do not need Dollars. Dollars need me.*"

Assume this mental attitude and see what a change it makes for you.

When you have changed your aura, Dollars will be drawn. You need not think of their coming, for they will come to you through the opportunities that this new mental attitude will reveal to you. Think only of using them.

MENTAL ATTITUDE TOWARD DOLLARS

Change your attitude towards the Dollars you have. Tell them they are of no use until they are expended.

As you see them lying about, say to them: "*Idle Dollars, go to work. Go out and circulate. Each one of you go and pay a million in wages and debts. When I need you, come back again. You are useless and have no value until you go to work.*"

Then LET them go to work, knowing that when you send this thought with them, they or their companions will come back to you to be set at work.

SPEND THE DOLLARS

Before you spend a Dollar, the question comes, "Is it right?" Whether you have a single Dollar, or whether behind the one you think of spending are a million, makes no difference.

If it is right to spend the Dollar in the proposed way, had you the million, it is right thus to spend this, the lone one.

Therefore, when you feel it is right to spend a Dollar for any purpose, spend it as royally as if you were a millionaire.

From the Inner Life, this message was given to me years ago: "*Let a thought of use stand guard over your purse and then spend freely.*"

Amend this by affirming: "*A thought of the righteousness of the spending stands guard over my Dollars and I send them forth with blessing.*"

THOUGHTS DO THE WORK

These Dollars, like every thought of good you send out, will return to bless you. You do business with thoughts only; Dollars are but materialized thoughts.

Each Dollar in any woman's hand represents her thought in material form.

Send out at all times with your Dollars the thoughts you wish to return to you, for what you sow in your Dollars, you reap in Dollars that either do, or do not, come back to you.

Put the thought of Success, Happiness and Health into every Dollar that passes out and it will return so laden.

POLES OF THOUGHT

Having acquired the proper mental attitude, there is something necessary for you to do to draw the Dollar.

Your magnet of desire must have two poles.

First, you must have something that the world needs and is willing to pay for. In this respect you must follow the law of supply and demand.

You must honestly feel that you will give the Dollar's worth for every Dollar that you desire.

Secondly, you must, in all sincerity, dedicate every Dollar that comes to you to noble service.

You can then feel that Dollars want you; that through them you can give what you have of value to the world.

Feel that Dollars wish you to use them for the

accomplishment of your purpose to use them justly. With this ideal, you can conscientiously invite Dollars and they will come. They need your heart, brain and hand that they may benefit the world.

WHAT ARE DOLLARS?

Dollars are manifestations of the One Infinite Substance as you are, but, unlike you, they are not Self-Conscious. They have no power till you give them power.

Make them feel this through your thought-vibrations as you feel the importance of your work. They will then come to you to be used.

They will not come, nor can you in this thought draw them, to be hoarded.

Use, helpfulness and happiness must be in your thought of success. This held firmly, perseveringly, as your affirmation, will turn the current of Dollars your way.

WHAT TO THINK

Your thought should be:
I possess that which the world wants.
Dollars want me to use them in scattering that which I have to bless.

Use these Affirmations persistently:

DOLLARS LOVE ME.
I AM READY TO USE DOLLARS AND THEY FREELY COME TO ME TO BE USED.

Make no limit as to the amount. Claim abundance.

CLAIM ALL YOU CAN USE FOR GOOD, all that is needed to enable you to be useful and happy.

TIME A FACTOR

In all your self-culture, you are to remember that time is a necessary factor in unfoldment.

It is not a measure of duration. This mistake of measuring time by the figures on a dial will never do in this culture.

Time is to be measured by growth. Some may grow more while the hands count twenty-four hours than others in ten times that.

Take no thought of time. You have all there is. You are Spirit (or Mind, if you prefer the word) and have all eternity.

Seeds require time to germinate, grow, leaf, bud, bloom, blossom and fruit. Each thought, each change in your ideal, is a seed. It will follow nature's line of evolution.

You will require time as you change your attitude! A period will be required to change your vibrations so that the Dollar will feel you and learn that it wants you.

This period will vary according to your power of concentration and your fidelity to your ideal as couched in the Affirmation:

Dollars want me.

The thought-field is first to be cleared of the weeds of the old thought-sowing and the seeds of the new must germinate and bear fruit in the Garden of Supply.

FORGET THE PAST

Pay no attention to the old conditions. Keep at your affirmation, knowing that it is the gate to the reservoir and every irrigating ditch will fill as soon as water can come down from the reservoir to it.

"*I Want!*"

The echo, "*I want Dollars,*" must become still before the real sound of *Dollars want Me* can vibrate in Your aura.

Know, as the merchant knows that she has that which the people want, that you have that which Dollars want.

In your thought, in your hand, in your life, advertise your purpose to the Dollar. Tell it that it wants all these; that without you, it has no power; that, without you, it can do nothing.

Tell it that all that it wants, you have; that it will come to you that it may accomplish its mission. Then like a patient merchant, wait for your customers.

Dollars will soon flock to you as do customers to a bargain counter. The "What Dollars Want Column" has attracted them.

Use here only the same commonsense, perseverance and patience the successful businesswoman uses and Dollars will find their wants supplied in you, and you will find your own Supply.

FUNDAMENTAL CONSIDERATIONS

CONSCOUSNESS OF WANT

"Creator hid the whole world in your heart," says Emerson.

This fact humans have taken long to perceive. From cave dwellers to twentieth century millionaires, the propelling force has been a consciousness of lack.

"*I want food,*" said primitive humans. This drove them to activity and led to their unfoldment, for it awakened in them a consciousness of the ability to supply that want. It led them to recognize the fact that food already existed. They did not, however, reach our higher viewpoint.

Neither has the twentieth century millionaire reached it, for she still shares that primeval ignorance and says, "*I want Dollars.*"

This little book is a call to her to leave that primeval attitude and come up onto this higher plane where she will hear the world's work calling to her: "*I want you.*"

NECESSITY, THE SPUR TO UNFOLDMENT

In the development of human necessity has been a big incentive. Necessity has driven the wheels of progress.

Animals also feel the spur of necessity. But there is in humans a plus - the imagination, a psychic quality, which has been a stronger factor in their development than has been animal necessity.

This power of imagination differentiates people from animals, lifts them above the animal plane and makes them human.

THE IDEAL

It was imagination that led cave dwellers to paint faces and to carve pictures on bones.

The Ideal, "*The haunting dream of the better,*" floating before the individual, has lured her on to thought and action.

From the animal matrix the power of the Ideal drew forth the human. Necessity drives, the Ideal draws. As the Ideal develops so does its power to draw develop.

When humans in their unfoldment shall have left the animal entirely behind, they will know no necessity, but will in all ways live from the ideal.

Then there will be neither necessity nor want. Brutes want; Woman has.

HUMAN POSSIBILITY

The Human Soul possesses potentially all possible power. Like heat in coal, this Power in Woman waits for expression. Power in coal or steam waits for opportunity for expression, but Woman makes her own opportunity.

POWER NEEDS WOMAN

As fast as Woman learns that the power in coal, electricity or radium waits for her to use it, she puts them to use, and learns that from all eternity they have waited for the thought necessary to direct them in work for her.

ALL THINGS AWAIT WOMAN'S THOUGHT

All progress is but a change of mental attitude toward conditions that exist. "*A weed is a plant people do not know the use of,*" says Emerson.

So the condition, whatever it be, that is today untoward, when a woman knows how to use it, will be found favorable.

There are millions of weeds waiting for her to learn their use. Weeds want her. They will tell their secret to her listening ear.

"*Weeds as well as roses live for our happiness.*"

THE IDEAL LEADS TO DISCOVERIES

Desire for something new led women to find colorful dyes in what were useless weeds; to find food in others and in others clothing and building material.

Plants, minerals and unknown forces are still waiting for her to use them.

Women are ever to think: "*NEW FORCES want me!*"

LOVE OF THE IDEAL

Love-for-the-ideal leads to desire. Desire leads to action. Action converts difficult conditions into the ideal.

In the old thought, a woman was controlled by "want." She was ignorant of her place and power in Nature.

In this thought of want she worked and labored. Yes, even in her spiritual life, she held the idea of the want of, the lack of, heaven.

But the fact is, heaven holds out rewards for her, because it desires her good.

WANT IS A LACK OF PERSONHOOD

Want is born from the non-intelligence of the undeveloped individual that women have not yet outgrown.

The individual woman, conscious of her power, does not want. She knows that whatever is needed for her health, happiness and unfoldment already is.

All she needs to know is where and how to get it.

The Psalmist said in a most matter-of-fact way: "*The Lord is my shepherd. I shall not want!*"

Why? Because the Power that called us into Being prepared conditions for us before we came.

Jesus saw the same truth in the realization that he was an integral portion of the universe. He said: "*I and my Divine Creator are one.*"

"*All things that the Creator hath are mine!*" And he

had learned how to get them. He could not lack. He knew his power. "*Even the wind and the sea obeyed him!*"

NATURE'S DEMAND

THINGS FOR WOMEN AND NOT WOMEN FOR THINGS!

Any woman who realizes this Truth cannot want. All Good desires her best, is constantly bidding for her, and even lying in wait for her.

Opportunities are ever present for her to use. Power and things that represent power are at all times present for her unfolding into consciousness of herself as Being; as a Daughter of Infinite Wisdom.

The constant enlargement of this consciousness causes a constant change of mental attitude, so that she learns to use opportunities and conditions instead of being used by them.

WORTH OF A WOMAN

When once a woman has reached this consciousness of herself, she realizes the value of Emerson's admonition: Let a person know her worth and keep things under her feet.

Let her not peep or steal, or skulk up and down

like a charity-girl, an orphan, or an interloper in the world that exists for her.

She will know that all that is, is for the unfolding into consciousness of the embryo Creator which she is.

FOLLOWING THE IDEAL

She will follow in love her Ideal, and there will constantly open fields of activity that desire her. There will constantly be more power asking her to harness it.

In power, she is finding now only the promise of future knowledge, a vaster use.

Power is an atmosphere that cannot be limited or lessened. In consciousness of herself as Power-to-use-power, a woman will not seek to possess things, but will learn to use things.

Thus will the Law be fulfilled---"Seek first the Realm of God, then will things be added!"

NO LIFE WASTE

This truth perceived, a woman will not waste life in hoarding and clinging to things. Each day she will use, in love, everything that is hers to use and thus will develop her power to draw other things that desire her to use them.

She will gradually unfold the ability to see and improve the incessant opportunities that present themselves to her.

She will come to know that Nature wants her thought and love to help her express Her latent forces, which are merely waiting for the hand of a woman to loose for her use.

Nothing has value save that which adds to a woman's health, happiness or usefulness.

INVENTIONS

The power of the inventions of Watt, Stephenson, Edison and Langly to revolutionize civilization is small compared with the transforming power flowing through the mental attitude expressed in the Thoughts:
"*Things want me!*"
"*Nature wants me.*"
"*Creator wants me!*"

POWER OF TRUTH

Every new perception of Truth causes changes in every line of thought and endeavor.

The Truth that women are WANTED will work a greater advancement in spiritual welfare than the perceptions of scientist and philosopher have wrought in material and intellectual good so far.

UNIVERSAL PRINCIPLE

The Principle is universal.

Each woman must entirely reverse her attitude toward Nature, herself, and things.

She must recognize that, as the crowning expression of Infinite Power, she is to accept her place as the ruler and she is to exercise dominion over all things.

She must affirm: "The world exists for me. It is for my use. It has no other use than to minister to me. Without me there is no purpose, no ultimate in Nature."

SOCIAL CHANGE

There can never be a happy and equitable condition in society until the present attitude of want is changed.

Whenever the masses shall affirm, '*Things want me!*" then the ideal will be near.

A woman will then see that she is infinite in her possibilities; that time and things are simply the means by which she comes into consciousness of her own divinity and immortality.

That change comes to each woman when she learns to affirm in Truth:

"*I possess!*" in place of, as she now says: "*I Want!*"

"*Dollars want me!*" in place of "*I want Dollars!*"

GREAT IS THE CHANGE

This change is so great that when proposed to the average woman, she no more sees the Principle and its import than would the child by Franklin's side have understood him, had Franklin said that the lightning which he was drawing from the sky would run streetcars and drive automobiles and airplanes.

"*Dollars want me!*" will work a no less marvelous change in the world's social life.

CRITICISM

I am aware that the principles of this little book are an easy mark for the humorous or satirical pen of the superficial critic.

Plain as my point of view is, the blind critic can easily miss it. And the point of view is all-important.

THE POSITION OF THE BOOK

I affirm the infinite possibilities of the human soul;. I have faith in every woman having power to overcome all limitations and to realize that she is able, through expressing her divinity, to have dominion.

She will have this as fast as she learns her power.

I affirm that there is but One Power, One Mind. All phenomena are but a manifestation of that One.

The self-conscious manifestation of that mind in her, because she is self-conscious, has power to command obedience from all that is not self-conscious, to command all that is not herself.

Money, being a part of All and also being a creation of human thought, is subject to a woman's will.

All this my critics may not accept, and consequently they will look from the old thought point of view. Having no thought in common, they cannot agree with me.

WORK AND PRACTICE

Do you wish to know the truth of these principles? Practice them and await results.

The final test is always "*By their fruits ye shall know them.*"

Practice is necessary. No ideal can be reached

without great effort. Your desire must be accompanied by earnest work. Indolence will never draw.

The magnet works or it would not draw the needle. Thought is work. Concentration and will and effort are necessary.

PLAN AND STICK TO IT

Accept the Principle and then, as the architect plans and concentrates on her work till her house rises complete, for otherwise it would be a medley, so you must build an ideal of opulence and stick to it, no matter what comes, until you actualize your ideal in the objective.

It is no easy task to develop the faith that moves Dollars. But it is easier than to endure the poverty.

Be as persistent in thinking and declaring, "*I am rich!*" as you have been in declaring, "*I am poor*".

With equal persistency say, "*I have Dollars!*" as you had been saying "*I want Dollars!*"

I will promise you that you will grow into that mental attitude of perception that will see and take advantage of opportunities to earn the Dollars that lie all about you now unperceived.

No woman can do her best under the thought of poverty, under a thought of want.

Knowing her ability, a woman does her best at her work. Under fear, doubt, or mistrust she can never do good work.

The successful woman knows she has the power and uses to best advantage the tools available to her.

It is always the mental attitude that determines success. Let that attitude be: "*Business wants me!*"

AN INSTANCE OF SUCCESS

A gentleman in my class in Boston who furnished a noon luncheon to hundreds said: "*Mr. Brown, I don't understand how!*"

"*Why did you select that location for your business?*" I asked.

"*Because it was in the center of the business district and there was opportunity for me!*" he answered.

"*Surely,*" said I, "*You have answered my question. You went there because business called you. Business wanted you. You said, "People want dinners and I go to furnish them."*

He saw the point, applied it, and thinking

thereafter, "People want dinners!", drew more customers and increased his business.

We radiate a mental atmosphere that is sensed and is potent. She who says, "*I want your Dollars!*" repels you. She who says, "*You want my goods and I am glad to serve you!*" draws business.

TALK TO YOURSELF

Treat yourself as teacher and pupil; as doctor and patient. With constraining directness make your affirmations to yourself.

Only thus can you open up the sources of infinite power that are within you. This talking is best done in formulas positively expressing I am!

AFFIRMATIONS FOR SUCCESS

The teachings of preceding pages have been necessary that you, my reader, may fully understand the Principle of Affirmation.

Now I will give you some examples in the way of Affirmations.

If you will repeat them until it becomes a habit for you to think along these lines of thought as automatically and persistently as you have along the old lines, it will so completely change your life expression that you will, in comparison with your past, seem like a new person.

WHAT TO AVOID

Avoid negative expressions.

Never use words that are not in line with your desire.

Here is an important expression to avoid:
I CAN'T AFFORD IT!

It is common when a person desires a thing and does not feel that she can expend the cash for it to say: "*I cannot afford it!*"

But what are the Dollars in your purse? To spend. Can you afford to spend them? Is it not that for which you have them? You do not mean that you cannot afford. This thought makes you the servant of the Dollar.

What you really mean is: "*I do not feel that this thing is the one I can best buy now. I prefer to use the Dollar in other ways.*" This is the proper attitude of mind. In it you continue to be the Master and the Dollar is subject to your decision.

This may seem like a very little thing. But it is the most important thought you can apply in your career for success.

It is "*Dollars want me!*" thought, and not the thought, "*I want Dollars to tell me what I shall do with them!*"

A gentleman once said to me, "*I'd like to buy some of your books, but I cannot afford it!*"
"*Excuse me,*" said I. "*You smoke ten-cent cigars?*"
"*Certainly,*" was his reply.
"*At least five a day?*"
"*Sure,*" he said.
"*You can afford them?*"
"*I do!*"

"Then you will pardon me. You should have said, 'I can afford to buy some books if I decide, but I prefer to spend the Dollar for cigars.'"

This is your privilege. Exercise your personal liberty and be master of your pocketbook and say, '*I spend the Dollar as I desire!*' *"I have spent so much!"*

This is another important idea: Have you spent money for something that represented value to you?

For example, you bought some nice clothes. Twenty Dollars, say, exchanged for new clothes. In taking account, instead of thinking of this as Dollars spent or gone, think of it as changing the twenty Dollars from cash assets to clothing assets. Your account balance is the same.

INVESTMENT

Another way to look at money expended is as an investment. If you invest five hundred Dollars in mining stock, you look for dividends. So invest every Dollar that passes out of your hands.

It is an investment in education, in health, in experience.

Feel this way toward the Dollars, as they go, and then your mental attitude will be so clear that you will see opportunities for other investments that will bring sure dividends.

Regret, sorrow, fears, remorse, and all such attitudes of mind so cloud the judgment that other effects similar to those regretted will follow.

Happy, peaceful, contented, trustful, and self-respectful mental states keep the reason, conscience and judgment clear and proper investments will be made under them.

Always see a dividend coming in from every Dollar that goes from your purse. The greatest of all dividends is experience, for it is ever afterward a mental asset that increases the value of every decision.

"I've lost so much!"

This expression is akin to the spending idea, but worse. Away with it!

The lesson learned is worth all it cost. Nature always gives measure for measure. So much experience for future guidance is always adequate recompense.

All one gets out of life is the result of experience.

Experience is the expression of life - the pressing

out of life into consciousness. All our present consciousness is the result of experience. The present is but adding, through experience, to the sum total of our consciousness.

So is it true that we act with all our past, and think in the present? For this reason, no one has any cause to regret, or repent, or be sorry for any experience. A woman is today, in consciousness, all that she has expressed of the infinite possibilities of the Soul.

Let her say: "*I have always expressed as my reason, my desire and my will have determined. I have learned by experience what expression brings happiness and what misery. According to my power to choose, to decide and to persist have I used the experience. Because of my use of Dollars I learn how to use them if I am wise. If I do not learn, then the want which I allow myself to feel for the Dollar will be the cause of more suffering!*"

Once a woman has mastered that want by realizing the principles set down in this book she will feel no sorrow over lost Dollars, for she will know that the Dollar spent, or the Dollar others call "lost," is hers as experience forever!

FINANCIAL FREEDOM

Financial freedom is the real desire that actuates a woman in her work for the Dollar.

That freedom will never come as long as she gives the Dollar any power to add to, or to detract from, her happiness.

Until she realizes that it is her attitude toward the use of the Dollar that will bring satisfaction, there will always be the cry of "*Want!*"

AFFIRMATIONS

I therefore recommend that the following affirmations be used until the mental attitude they express becomes habitual:

I

I desire a deep consciousness of financial freedom.
I desire that the flow of prosperity become equalized.
I desire a greater consciousness of my power to attract the Dollar.
I desire a constant success in my business.

II

When you have used these until you are conscious of a definiteness in your desire, you may use the following:

I have a deeper consciousness of financial freedom.
I am financially free. "Dollars want me."
The Indwelling Power cares for in my wallet.
I have whatever I desire.
I have no question of expenditure. What I feel I need, that I purchase.

I can afford to use Dollars for my happiness.
I have clothes, food, books, entertainment and whatever I need for health, happiness, friendship, and service to others.

III

Here is another that was developed with the assistance of a friend for me in a time of my own weakness:

I MUST ALWAYS SAY TO MYSELF-
"*I AM financially free.*"
I must see to it that the two women, the material and the spiritual that I am, blend to the purpose of financial success.
I see myself in such a financial condition that the money is always there – actually there - to use, freely and in fullness.

I always have a full bank account. I actually see it.

My one idea of the Law is to use, use, USE.

I insist rigidly upon using my Law most persistently, until I have my full demonstration.

I have strength of character, stamina, backbone, powerful purpose in accomplishing.

I demonstrate that I'll have my home, funds for business, for recreation, and for any improvement in myself.

I affirm:
Real emancipation.

Real freedom to make the very best in my life.

THE HONEY POT

Now I never weaken my position by affirming that I want anything. I say it wants me, and I know it will come.

It is not any use making that statement, of course, if you DOUBT IT. You must back up your statement with faith and feel it is already yours.

It is rather on the principle of the honey pot and the swarm of summer flies; you are the pot of honey - the Dollars are the flies.

Now the honey doesn't worry about the flies, it is content to be sweet, to give off a faint sweet smell and to stick, but the flies do want, they come from all quarters, they swarm into it, sip its sweetness, and buzz-zz-zz all around. The honey is a power - irresistible power so far as flies go - they want, it is a great center of attraction.

Now, say you run some particular line of business - you are the honey - in the world there are many people who want what you have to give them, who will gladly pay cash for it, who cannot help being attracted to your honey, as the flies might be.

THOUGHT IS POWER

Your thought is strong and potent beyond measure, but when you assume the wanting attitude, although you do most certainly attract, it is nothing like the powerful attraction formed by your quiet, confident attitude of absolute conviction that the thing *wants you*.

The attitude of desire is strong, but the attitude of certainty - of possession - which this new thought makes possible is wonderful, and a veritable tower of strength; it has made things possible to me that were quite out of the question before.

THE END

ABOUT THE AUTHOR

Henry Harrison Brown was born in Massachusetts in 1840, and served in the U. S. Volunteers during the Civil War. He taught school, worked with newspapers, and lectured in various fields for 17 years and was a Unitarian minister for 7 years. In 1900 he founded the New Thought publication, NOW and continued writing and lecturing until his death in 1918.

ABOUT THE TRANSCRIBER

Sarah Anne Shockley has been a student of metaphysics for over 40 years and is the author of multiple books published by Any Road Press and New World Library. She has an MBA in International Business and is a Master Practitioner of Transformational NeuroLinguistic Programming, working with private clients worldwide. She lives in Northern California.**www.SarahAnneShockley.com**

www.WomensNewThoughtLibrary.com

Made in the USA
Monee, IL
04 November 2026

67377683R00030